I, Machete

POEMS

D0882309

ALSO BY MADHURI PAVAMANI

The Keeper Series (adult urban fantasy)

Dutch

Juma

Death

The Sanctum Trilogy (paranormal romance)

The Girl

The Boy

The Prophecy

The Survival Files (MG fiction)

Crossin' Paths

Tough Times

for the warriors
be angry, be loud
love hard and live fast

we are the magic

CONTENTS

I. EPHEMERA

II. LIMERENCE

III. EPIPHANY

I.

EPHEMERA

Some things come with their own punishments.
- Arundhati Roy

Lessons

It's okay to admit I loved you
and perhaps on some stratum,
you loved me too
once upon a time
or for a few beats of
our togetherness, and
it wasn't a bad thing
you and I
the fact we happened
the whole of us was not
dysfunction and deceit
there were small bursts of bright
light and laughter, stars and epic moonsets
for a brief wondrous moment
we felt anything but ephemeral

Queen Me

when you think of me
I hope I'm the warrior queen
in our battle of souls
because I gnashed my teeth
clawed your skin and
bellowed to the moon
when I professed
myself to you

        if only I'd known

              your kingdom

          lay elsewhere

Maps and Plans

what does your
escape plan
look like?

how did you
disappear with
such ease?

if there's a
part of you
I wish you'd shared

it's the map
you drew
to freedom

Yes and No

every YES
I have spoken
in this crazy love
has your name etched
all over them
each NO
you have uttered
is made up
of me

I Still Have Hope for You

one day
may you grow
into a version of yourself
I am able to roll
around in my mouth
without gagging on the taste
of your duplicity

Care Package

a package arrived in the mail today
perfectly wrapped and tied
in polka dot paper and pretty string
and I knew it was from you
because you know I love all things dotted
and boxes tied with string
remind me life is full of surprise
and inside, nestled on a soft pillow
of silvery tissue rested my heart
intact but barely beating
horribly bruised
battered and scarred
with a note attached
in your perfect script:

RETURN TO SENDER

and perhaps another girl
would rant and lose herself
in the loss of you
but I told you
time and again
I am not like other girls
so thank you for the care package
I want my heart
I rather like it

and believe one day
someone else will, too
I appreciate the time you took
wrapping it just so
it's back in my chest
learning to beat anew

Song

There is a Lenny Kravitz song
that opens with a drum roll
and then moves into all kinds of sexiness
in that narrow hips
leather pants
big dick
rockstar way
that only Lenny can do
and it reminds me of that summer
when I breezed into that store
and I spied you
and you moved into my space
like you knew me
and I started to say
what the
because I'm not the kind of girl
you get all up on
but the words
got trapped somewhere
in the web of your masculine perfection
and before I knew it

we were at dinner
laughing like we'd known each other
forever
when really

all we knew
was we wanted each other
now
we tumbled into your apartment
an amalgam of arms
legs
lips
tongues
until I caught my breath
and said *stop*

your hands cupped my ass
my legs wrapped your waist
our bodies pressed the wall
hot breath
the only sound in the silence
and I wondered why I suddenly became
the girl who didn't on the first date
when I was always the girl
who did whatever she pleased
you gathered yourself and smiled
because under all that smoldering sex
you were the consummate gentleman

I'm gonna put on some music
grab yourself a drink
and just like that
our dance
was back on
this time more subtle

tentative
full of seduction
as Lenny and that rhythm
so sexy and quiet
urgent and low
settled in our blood
pooled in our bones
and did things to us

whispered stories
nervous laughter
the touch of my knee
the warmth of your mouth
my fingers learned your scars
you traced my ink
bit by bit
painstaking
stripped naked
and vulnerable
brown on more brown
curves and hard planes
stilled breath
parted lips
beautiful
young
and in lust

That was a lifetime ago
the summer we found each other
when your hands learned

every inch of my body
your mouth devoured me
and your beautiful mind
captured my soul
holding me hostage
forever

We were so young
as we parted
still listening to Lenny
laughing about all kinds of forever-evers
I-love-you-no-matter-whats
we-got-this you-wait-and-see
little did we know
there would be a late night
a car
and a gun
because we were young
and in love
and believed darkness didn't touch
kids like us

Until it did.

So yeah
there is a Lenny Kravitz song
that opens with a drum roll
then moves into all kinds of sexy shit
it reminds me of our summer
and you

and love

And I hate that damn song.

Mad Skills

you are so good
at making me
not miss you
at all

Realization

if nothing about you
inspires words
then perhaps
you are not love
after all

Scars

I stiffen at a raised voice
gut churns and
bile fills my throat
when I consider the possibility
of others in my personal space
will they understand all
the ways I might hesitate
and the bodies I must protect
will they hear me when
I say no, not tonight, or ever
will they trust I love deeply
just in my own way
my own time
I stiffen at a raised voice...

Whole Lotta

there was
a whole lot
of heaven
in his intentions
but damn
he left me feeling
like hell

Fool

do you
know
late
at night
when
all
is so still
even the
leaves
sleep
and
the wind
takes a
breather
when
the quiet
creeps
into
the dark
spaces
and
solitude
is
spelled
with a
capital

S

I crawl

forth

from my

bed

fingers

raw and bloody

as I

escape my

self-imposed

grave

of

missing you

and

stalk

the night

in

search

of your

scent

your essence

your soul

and

nothing

quells

my crave

no wine

no water

only you

I call out

in despair
my cries
falling
on
deaf ears
and
still I
seek
you
my one
true love
my only
my heart
and
I know
I am
doomed
to forever
roam
these streets
in search
of you
incapable
of touching
another
as when my
fingers
traced the
lines
etched into

your skin
but
I care
not
and I
know
you
will never
love
me as
you do
she
that your
words
are not
promises
they
are mere
sounds
pushed together
uttered in
the moment
meaningless
no matter
how much
meaning
I read
into them
but I
care not

and trust

when

death

calls me

home

nothing will

keep

me from

you

I shall

prowl

city

sidewalks

and

alleys

in search

of you

my one

true love

my only

my heart

still incapable

of accepting

your

rejection

of us

still

willing

to play

dumb

in the face
of your
perfection
still
yearning
for the sweet
of your
breath
and the
soft of
your sigh
forever
shamed
by the
fact
when I
wasn't
looking and
my guard
was down
love snuck up
from behind
and made
me her
fool

Love Games

when I kiss you
I taste him
and when you
touch me
his fingertips
already claimed my skin
he owns my sighs
my heart beats his name
Is that what
you want to know?
my ugly truths
dark and cold
and graffitied
with his initials
or should we keep
pretending at this love?

Notes of an Affair

I wrote you so many words
my frenzied soul
reduced to scratch
on pieces of paper
crumpled in your bag
and forgotten

I don't regret
sharing my deepest
secrets and dreams
I only wish I'd kept
a few of those notes
for myself

as poignant reminders
in this game of souls
to beware and use caution
the next time
I feel the itch
to roll the dice
and take a chance
on love

Signs

if the tender
of my kiss
tastes like
goodbye
it is because
you should
have fled
long ago

Onward

you are my
first thought
when I open
my eyes
but I'm learning
to dream of others
each time
they close

The Damnedest Things

This train reeks of bodies flush with coffee freshly made up faces
and the stress of let-me-get-to-my-meeting-on-time. Rush Hour,
when earbuds are in and lips yawn the morning awake and no
one looks at anyone but I see him, legs crossed and head down,
jamming a toothpick between his teeth like he and that wood got
some things to work out, and any other morning I would cringe
and turn inward at all the personal grooming that should take
place in the privacy of one's home but instead happens right out
in the open. Such is big-city living. and that nastiness makes my
skin crawl, all you mascara-applying, teeth-picking, nail-cutting
weirdos. But not today. Today I watch that man work his teeth,
every in-and-out, dip-between-the-gums, dig-out-the-gunk, and
I'm mesmerized. All that grotesquerie is reminiscent of you.
Pieces of rot to make up a deceptive whole. "No one will ever
love you like I do." The train lurches and wheels screech, tooth
man loses his pick, I grab for the overhead bar. And you are
forgotten. Balance. Little else matters.

When All Else Fades

even now
when I sit and ponder
your disavowal
of all things us
I cannot imagine
anything but
loving you

The Weight of Diamonds

the women next me on this
train ride to somewhere
click clack on their computer keyboards
as the garish diamonds on their ring fingers
glint in the sunlight streaming
through the car windows
why do we call them ring fingers
I wonder as I try and block out
the frantic sound of their typing
and business chatter, the lilt of their
accentless voices
where must one come from
to sound so anywhere, I think
to myself in language that reeks of
red clay far below the Mason Dixon
lazy slow like I got time
on my side and nothing matters
when all I can think about are those rings
and their relationships
and it does matter
not that I am a diamond girl, and
could I ever commit
he would be the kind of man who knew
better than to buy a bauble for my hand
(he would be you)
but the love trips me up because

I am a mess
and as much as I want to be the
woman who invites you into her heart
and home, and shares your bliss
sparks your joy
says *here's a copy of my key* and
your toothbrush is next to mine
I balked last night when you asked
how to lock up my place, and every time
I say I love you, and you say it back
my heart flutters
not in a good way, but like those
birds who beat against a cage
to escape, their wings moving a
mile a minute, their eyes wild,
and all of them focused on one thing:
how do I get out of here?
I want to be soft with love and wrapped
in a sweet caress, but I cannot let go and
leap into the void of faith and trust, so
I am steel nails and defy logic
I love you but don't love me back
I am a mess
and left to contemplate
those women and their rings
and how careless they seem
about all that weight wrapped
around their fingers, don't they
know love like that steals bits of
the soul, how come they don't worry

about losing themselves to the
whims of another
the flights of fancy
the terrible mind
I read love poems and think
on romance, and try to fill
up up up
with all kinds of magic
and tenderness and convince
myself that the pretty story
everyone falls for and re-reads
again and again and again
has a place for me and a
place for you and we are seated
together at the table of forever
and I am safe in this cocoon
you spool, but somewhere between
I love and you exist beats of time
I can't get back if I
should ever dare
to throw caution to the wind
and give them to you
the man who touches me like
I am precious and
without a sound tells me
there is none more
beautiful that I
am his everything
and I pause and shake
because as much as I love

you and this dream we
keep trying to build together
the one that looks like
late nights in bed
pancake breakfasts
afternoon hikes endless
hours exploring all the
things we are curious about
chatter laughter
a kiss
I cannot break the cycle and
believe there is freedom
in the palm of your hand should
I be so brave to take it
because I see those diamonds
and the weight of love and
I am a mess

II.

LIMERENCE

Love makes your soul crawl out from its hiding place.

- Zora Neale Hurston

War

love
in these times
of despair is
revolution
hold my hand, baby
let's start this
war

Who Are You and What Have You Done with My Good Sense?

you make me want
all of the things
I never believed in

Can We Do This Again and Again Forever?

when our paths diverge
and you turn to leave
there's moonshine
trapped in my chest
my gut is a pool
of soft laughter
breath stills
and I'm already
waiting

Gentle the Dreamer

I dreamt you last night
in my space without
invitation, no warning
turned around and
there you stood
explaining yourself
all the wheres whys hows
of your presence
because you know
my panic buttons and how
sometimes the slightest gestures
feel like violence, smell like blood
you were disheveled and soft
and your voice, its rhythm
and cadence felt like
home, and when I woke
kissed by sunlight creeping
through the window slats
all of me felt gentle

Say My Name

my name
on his
lips
is
Elysian

Writing

there are beautiful words
in the brown of
your skin
let me kiss them
and make sweet poetry

The Resistance

fire is my blood
moonlight kisses my fingertips
as the forest echoes and sighs
these veins of mine
deep and intricate
full of cool water and time
find you
warm to my chill
whiskey to my wine
heart of my heart
tonight let us be still
quiet
entwined
love is our resistance

Beautiful Girl

inspired by the wondrous Frida Kahlo

You deserve a lover who stills when you enter a room
stunned by your mischievous eyes and gap-toothed smile
who finds beauty in your imperfections
and makes you forget you ever considered them so

You deserve a lover who wakes you in the middle of the night
with poetry on his tongue and fire in his fingertips
who kisses you to sleep
and fills your mornings with strong coffee and witty banter
who craves you 24/7 and isn't shy about saying it

You deserve a lover who is messy and laughs loud and laughs
often
who holds your hand and sings Nina Simone off-key
who is serious about politics and papermate flair tip pens
and dragons and the environment
but mostly is serious about you

You deserve a lover who listens to your quiet and lets it swallow
you whole
who is okay when you disappear and upon your return
waits with a whiskey and a filthy joke
who understands no matter what
you will always come back

You deserve a lover who revels in slow Sunday mornings spent
together in bed

who reads you a snippet from The New Yorker on adulting and
ice cream
who snorts when he laughs as he teases you about snoring
then kisses you simply because he cannot help himself

You deserve a lover who gathers up your hurts in a bag for safe-
keeping
and brings you tulips and Bukowski and crossword puzzles
instead
who kisses away your tears and tickles your fancy
who fears not your darkness and dances away your blues

You deserve a lover who recognizes your vulnerabilities
as pieces of you that make up the whole
who celebrates your tiniest victories and
lifts you up on his shoulders in the face of defeat

You deserve a lover who looks at you like you matter
and then whispers the same into your curves and hollows
who knows your ugliest self and invites her to dinner every
Tuesday night
who met your banshee and introduced you to his wildling

You deserve a lover
who promises kisses
and laughter and truth

You deserve a lover
whose everything
is
you

On Feasts and Freedom

feed me freedom
she whispered
I need to know
I can come and go
as I please, when I want
and you won't despair my absence
you won't fear my disappearance
you will understand
the food of love
is a meal
best eaten
with a smile in my eyes
laughter on our tongues
and kisses made of honey

I will indulge your
every desire
to drift and roam
he replied
I will gather carpets of stars
and blankets of moonbeams
for the nights you are gone
I will wash well-trodden paths
and chop treacherous terrain
for a soup to nourish
your ever-meandering soul

I will milk the heavens
and knead the canyons
to bake your
wanderlust bread

so long as you allow me
to fall in love with you
he promised
I will feed you freedom
wrapped in parchment paper
and tied with a string

please
she replied
fall head over heels for me
make me fat
with love
then set me free
I promise to return

Privilege

there is privilege
lying here between us
and I do not mean
the you-are-privileged-
to-be-lyin'-here-
next-to-me type
I mean New York City
fancy job
fancier life privilege
I mean down South
acres of land
you don't want to debut?!
privilege
I mean yes we are brown
but our stories
trend white type
and I don't know
how that's got you feeling
but I do know
you the first one
I lie next to and
curl around and
none of it matters
we just us
and I don't know
where we'll be

tomorrow
or next month
or next year
but I do know
right now
we just us
and my god, what a
privilege it is

Logophilia

I glanced your way
and everywhere
I saw poetry

Full Circle

bodies stretched
pressed
skin to skin
heartbeats dance off-rhythm and
it sounds like release and wonder
breath and sigh and...

pause

they call this epiphany
this quiet magic

the moment I know

it's for you
I've been waiting

to you I belong

Snellville, Georgia

I'm a sucker for a man with a twang - this one's for y'all

his voice
like gravel and honey
curved around
her throat
caressed all her
tender spots
and in the quiet
of their togetherness
reminded her
of home

Like Beyoncé and Jay-Z (Drunk In Love)

no alcohol
gets me drunk
like you

On Panties and Books

when he says
he loves to read
it probably means
he wants to get
inside your panties
but also
that he loves to read
so maybe try him on
see what he's like
curl up next to him
and read a book

The Small Hours

During the blackest of night
the quietest of early morn
the words arrive furious and demanding

They scramble over each other
like small children
with arms and legs akimbo
fighting for attention
needing to be seen
heard
caressed

I ponder them as they spill forth
my page covered
and smile as I think of you
and the night we lay next to each other
you deep in my words
me lost in my head

I turned your way
to catch your gaze
full of quiet wonder and mirth

What? I whispered
you kissed me and smiled
The small hours suit you

your mysterious reply
Now as I write
in the dark solitude
of my haven
I hear your voice again
and all of me feels love

Indeed
the small hours suit me

Intemporel

Us
We feel timeless
and when I
look back in wonder,
it's as if
I knew
all along
you
were
coming

Crackle and Boom

roll through me
with your love
like a slow-moving
thunderstorm
dark and dangerous
coloring everything
with your ethereal hue
where the air feels
like a soft kiss
pressed to the inside of
my wrist
time stands still
and we're kids again
counting down
one Mississippi
two Mississippi
three

My Favorite Poem

it cannot be helped
even when I don't
want it to happen
it does

I cannot look upon you
without seeing poetry

the most beautiful rhythms
and movement
of words and meaning
together
commingled
in a perfect
thump-thump
like the beat of my heart
when your lips
trace the curve of my throat
and touch my soul
in tenderness and heat
the poetry of
love and touch
you and I
wrapped around each other
one
you are my poem

an endless amalgam
of all that is
good and
bad and
ugly
everything I love
the bits of you
I hold close
when we're apart
the seconds I count
until we are
together
again
your name dances along
my lips
curves around my waist
and kisses my toes
you thrum a beat
in my blood
that words try to capture
but only my heart
truly hears
you captivate me
always
blushed remembrances
of words shared
promises made
love
my favorite sounds
uh-huhs oh yeahs

please don't stops
live within your fingertips
your smile
in your presence
poetry becomes vivid and
demanding
necessary
where all I crave
is to find meaning
in the wonder of us
the poetry
love

I cannot look upon you
without it happening

you are
my favorite poem

Wild Love

be gentle
with me
he whispered
she smiled
and asked
or what?

Fire Escape

Those guys on the corner of 15th street
and 8th avenue
the ones selling weed cocaine ecstasy
really anything the white kids want
they're gorgeous
mindblowingly hot
and they move like sex
as I sit on my fire escape
and watch them do their dirty

Those women wrapped around each other
under the low street light
Her hand on her hip
and her lips on her throat
pressed against each other
so turned on
They live above me
and later tonight
she'll be crying
while she's beating her with
whatever she can get her hands on
and I'll be sitting here on my fire escape
listening to it all

That guy right there
the skinny one with his hand above his eyes

blocking out the sun
track marks on his arm
I know him
we're friends and I love him to death
but he's an addict
and has started shooting up again
and I just bought this television
and those books
so I'm going to keep sitting on my fire escape
and pretend I don't see him

You
with your long eyelashes
and big eyes
your tragic soul
and beautiful mind
who fought me tooth and nail
because you wanted to paint
and I wanted you out of my space
for two goddamned seconds

Come over here
with those hands that know my body
and those lips that are all kinds of danger
let's hang on my fire escape
and forget everything but each other

Deadly Things

come here
and let me be
your dying wish

Pretty Woman

I saw a man today
with the night sky in his eyes
and a soul full of stars,
and I wanted to slip inside his skin to see
if I could find the source of his magic
instead
I listened to the rhythm of his laughter
and thrilled at the slow curve of his words
and wondered where he learned to kiss like that,
pressed against the wall and breath stolen so fast
I forgot to remember all the things one thinks
when being kissed by true love

He stepped back and crooked-smiled
and then swallowed my hesitation
with the soft of his mouth,
and without uttering a sound
I knew he learned
the bloody edges of my fears,
and when I parted my lips to sigh in regret
because I wanted to be everything
unbroken for him me us,
all I heard was the sweet of his promise.

Don't worry pretty woman, he said slow and sure
and there was eternity in his everything
I got this, baby

John Waters Would Approve

I could lie
under an obsidian sky
all night with you
our books
and love

Moonstruck

I always loved the sun
until one night the moon
kissed my toes
and sang me a song
of time
tenderness
sweet soothing solitude
and I couldn't help
but wrap myself
around his silver sorcery
and fall for all of
his midnights

If I Could Write Poetry

if I could write poetry
it would be a love letter to the
curve of your neck
when you tilt your head to the side
and study something wondrous
I don't know if I could
make it more beautiful
than right now
when it's spoken in the moment
and your eyes dance with laughter
but I would try
I would put to verse
the sound of your voice
that slow sexy drawl and
how it curves around all of my edges
and makes everything
soft and sensuous
an exercise in futility
but wholly worth the effort
I would capture multitudes of stars
lighting dark earthen paths
deep in the forest
where we danced naked that night
and laughed like no one could hear
because they could not
the night belonged solely to

you me and our bliss
If I could write poetry
I would say all of those things
and it would be beautiful

Sweetheart, she sighed
and brushed his lips
with a kiss,
you just did

Small Things

It's a strange space to be
to think on another every day
desire them in ways unfathomable
and then walk through the world
as if they are an everyday kind of
thing, when really, they are the most
wondrous collection of atoms and matter
and life you've encountered and
if you could, you would wake to see
their beautiful eyes and sweet smile
each sunrise, you would lie down
together every night under a blanket
of stars, you would celebrate
in all kinds of small ways
the simple miracle
of their existence

Meditations

I want to lie on a carpet of
green grass with you,
stare at a star-filled sky and
say a quiet prayer of thanks
to the gods of love and chance
for their belief in the perfect
imperfection of us. And when you turn
my way and the grass tickles your cheek,
and that softness makes you want to
twine your legs with mine and pull me
close, but instead you catch my eye
and say what? please know, every second
in your space is a peaceful meditation,
you center me in love and memory,
and the curious curve of my mouth
is my soul singing on high

III.

EPIPHANY

today, I am a cold country, a
storm brewing, a heat wave of a woman
wearing red pumps to the funeral
of my ex-lover's
- Mahogany Brown, Litany

Tremendous

sweet girl
do not try to
break your bones
and become
small for another
bones heal
and you were always
larger than life

Once Upon A Time A Woman...

there is a story
hidden in the curve
of my hip
and the arch of
my foot
my ankle has
brushed death
old terrors rest in the
column of my spine
waiting for an opportune
moment to rise up
and shout
"Don't you forget me!"
I am told the body
holds trauma
in its memory cells
but I have no desire
to be its dark vessel
why must women always
bear the demons of
their menfolk
I fled that devil's nest
but carry its thorns
do not ask why I left
simply marvel
at my leap
to freedom

Axe and You Shall Receive

I once gave a lover a picture
of an axe, and excitedly
exclaimed *I want this!*
It was a beautiful thing,
the handle curved and
sanded just so, you knew
your fingers would wrap
around the wood and feel
right at home, the bladed head
honed and sharp, every inch
cried power. He took one
look at it, kissed me, and
laughed. Then he bought me
that axe, delivered with a bow
and a note in his scrawl:
my love, my tempest
may the world
forever know,
you are deadly

Some Girls

I am the madness of
a hot Southern night
                    when whiskey kisses
                            and honeysuckle sighs
                    shatter the silence
            and poets dream
                    impossible possibles
 when fingers twine
in crave-soaked sheets
            and a lover's
laughter   sings   like
                the
wind

Possession

first and foremost
I
belong
to
me

Deadly Weapon

those girls made of
sugar and spice and
everything nice
we were never friends
and they wouldn't know
whiskey from water
the way a jump shot
kisses the fingertips
long summer days
on a backwoods river

those girls are wife material
bring home to mama types
kiss goodnight sweethearts

I am a machete

Change of Address

this change of address
is like a welcome
shedding of skin
as I peel back
years upon years
of otherness
to find me
hidden under all the nonsense
waiting with a sly grin
a dirty joke
and the one
question that matters:
*what took you
so long, sweetheart?*

Obstreperous Me

all I managed
today
was to
color
outside
the lines

Grocery List

Tell me
is there a grocery store
for coming into yourself
perhaps called
Discovery Mart
or Second Acts Are Us?
are the aisles stacked
high and neat
with bottles of condensed humor
and skim degradation?
because whole degradation
was for that past life
and I'm on a diet these days
can I find packets of
twenty-four hour confidence
jars of self-love
belly-laugh frozen dinners?
lately those are my favorite
I could eat them every night
will I find fresh inner peace
and some ripe self-worth
situated next to the
red strawberries and green apples?
does the silence smell
as good as it looks?
I hope so

because I've got a list
crumpled in my pocket
and I'm headed there now
to refill my cabinets
and revel in this
rebirth

Women

I
am
amazed
by
the
wonder
of
us

The Unruly Girls

Shhhh
take off your shoes
slip out your window
and meet me in the forest
all the unruly girls
will be there
dancing
laughing
wilding.

Join us.

We
are
the
magic.

Epiphany

my god
you
are
a
gift

Freedom

how strange it is
to walk these paths
and think
where do I belong?
will anyone claim me,
attest I was here,
insist I mattered?

freedom is both a
most lovely and lonely shroud
to be donned
by the determined of heart
and fierce of spirit

I am learning
to slip her on and
wear her with pride

New Dawn

I can hear her breathing
so close
but just out of reach
the warmth of her
inhale exhale
excites and inspires
pushes me to rise each day
and do the things
small things
big things
scary things
she whispers in my ear
come sweet girl
let's rise
let's matter
I can hear her breathing
so close
but just out of reach
trust
I am coming

oh yes
I am coming

The Search

I looked for you
the other night
in cafes and pubs
searched back alleys
and lamp-lit park benches
until I got so lost
I forgot about you
and found myself
instead

Curve

your smile
is poetry in motion

Wings

once upon a time
she believed
loving him was freedom
then she fell
in love with herself
and soared

Wondrous Women

perhaps we should come
with warning labels:
watch out for us
we are fire and rage
honey and wine
we hang the stars
moonsets live on our tongues
the night sky hums with
our sighs
we are unmapped paths
through forests
the ones they warned you
not to traverse
but you did so anyway,
and now it cannot be helped
you are lost in us
forever

Girl Bodies

at fourteen this body felt like a prison
made of cordlike sinew and too-thick muscle
baby fat brown skin wishing for that Lisa Bonet pale
lips wide and full and nothing like a white girl's blossomed
in my
twenties
roared in bearing gifts of size 26 Levi's-skinny, coffee, cigarettes,
and New York City nights filled with
friends and dancing and white-girl-wannabe dreams no longer
mattered because yeah, life
rolled into
my thirties
were a tequila-fueled blur
if I'm going to be honest
and I am
that somehow someway
slipped into big-bellied-beyond-belief
(seriously, I gained 65 pounds)
knocked-upedness
soon-to-be mommy
(who me? yeah, you girl)
womanhood standing on the cusp
of forty
toes twinkling lips grinning
let's do this already, bring it on, life!
YES

LET'S
in all caps
thank you very much
says my almost-forty-seven years self
as I revel in
this brown skin dark eyes big nose wide smile gap tooth got-a-
butt-for-an-Indian-girl body
kiss my calamities
love up on my wild
I wish I celebrated your resilience and fortitude and every inch
of your brown magic before I knew such a thing existed
I wish I hugged my twenty-five year old thighs and rubbed my
thirty-two year old belly more often than I cursed them into
submission
non-existence
oblivion
I wish I looked at you the way Barack does Michelle
like love is all that matters every inch of my body is perfection
right down to my weird baby toes
like I am
enough.
I didn't then
I do now.

The Thief

last night
the stars focused
on the moon
the moon seemed awash
in memories of the sea
and the sea growled when
I sought her solace
so I stole
a cup of sky
and a handful of aurorae
wrapped my heart
in a blanket
of soft light
and promised
to try again
tomorrow

Revelation

I like you
but I like me more

In Repair

the woman
you admire from afar
with her back straight
voice strong
and laughter like
a summer breeze
I, too, see her
and wonder
what dark does she
hold in the curve of her smile
do her demons have names
and is that blade under her pillow
forever sharp
because please know
you don't get all that might
that heart
that fortitude
without a terrible fight

a phoenix can
only rise from
the ash

Untitled

these feet that readily
dance walk run
are just now discovering
balance
how to rest toes and heel
in a way the body
grounds solid to this
earth.

there is still shifting to
be done
a waiver
maybe even a fall.

but I'm getting there.

I am becoming.

It's Not An Either/Or Game

her dreams
are not to be deferred
to your desires

My Girlfriends, My Wives

white wine
whiskey
good food
and laughter

nights in your space
fill my life with light

Art Class

she always knew
he would break her
and from the
scattered pieces
she would gather herself
and make
beautiful art

To the Good Night

do not go gentle
into that good night
she said
so I roared my arrival
slayed some dragons
ravaged the menfolk
and danced in the forest
with my girls

it was loud and raucous
and full of abandon

it was twinkling lights
and moonsets

it was evermore

and my oh my
it was a
good night

Arsenal

Sweet girl,
unfurl your cool
blanket of indifference
slip into that
sublime cloak of
memory
and seek new truths
in the shards of
your soul
broken and tossed
carelessly
to the wind.

Those pieces of
time and love
meld into
a magnificent
sword.

Drag it across
the throat
of your demons.

Slay your dragons.

Roar.

Run!

If he says
no one will ever
love you
like I do
and it feels
like violence
and all things dark
trust your gut
and believe
it is okay
to say no
push back
with gnashed teeth
and bloody fingernails
ready to fight, to flee
His love
is not freedom
within lives no light
it is a vice
meant to shackle
and ground you
to him eternal
Run, my sweet, run!

Big Bigger Biggest

Can we skip the
small talk
and dive
head first
into the last time
you cried
words that move you
the weight of the moon
filigree butterfly wings?
Can we plot the revolution
discover a cure for cancer
foment economic stability
strangle the prison pipeline?
Can we do everything
big
bigger
biggest?
Can we?
Please.
Let's!

Healing

to the girl inside
who never felt heard,
for years
knew little tenderness,
and lived in fear:
you are safe now
I hear you
soar

Sanctify

In the practice of yoga, they ask you to set an intention before you begin. My intention with this collection is to elate. soothe, stupefy. If I come anywhere close, then I shall consider this endeavor a success.

And now, some thanks. Because books never happen alone.

Michele, Rafferty, Johnalynn, Christine - to laughter. And antics. And love, always love. The Rhode Island Writers Colony, and Miss Dianne and John Stephenson and Jason Reynolds - thank you. THANK YOU. For giving us the space to spread out and breathe and be, with our people, and our words. Anna de la Rosa, for all the baby steps you've guided me through this year - this book would still be sitting in my brain if it wasn't for my weekly sessions with you. Kimberly Brower, for your patience, and your whole-hearted belief in the power of my words. I couldn't ask for a better agent. My Girl Gang, my warriors, my loves. We are the magic, you are my sword. Christine, Adam, Danielle - thank you for reading my early drafts, without your guidance and encouragement this book wouldn't be in the wild. For mom. For dad. Look, no sex and barely any curse words. For my people: Ashok and Arsha, Preeya and Jawanza, Zeta, Jai, and Zara. For my hearts: Dash and Sydney. For smokey whiskey and difficult women. Poets and drunks. Blood and lust. For machetes. Lovers. And love.

About

MADHURI PAVAMANI writes things. Here and there, she reads them aloud. A daughter of the South - as in South India and the very small southern town of Snellville, Georgia - she is a practicing attorney in New York City and a 2017 resident of the Rhode Island Writers Colony. When she's not reading or writing or hanging with The Kid, she's probably somewhere upside down, practicing her handstands. You can follow her on Instagram and Twitter at @madhuriwrites.

JOHNALYNN HOLLAND is a multidisciplinary artist and writer from Emporia, Virginia. She holds a B.A. in Media Arts from The Atlanta College of Art and attended Howard University's Graduate Film Program. She was an artist-in-residence at the Taller Portobelo Norte of Portobelo, Panama, a writer-in-residence with the Rhode Island Writers Colony of Warren, RI and a Screenwriting Fellow with the ABC/Disney New Talent Development Program.

Notes

Notes

Read

More

Poetry

I, Machete

POEMS

CPSIA information can be obtained
at www.ICGtesting.com
Printed in the USA
FFHW021703110819
54191199-59941FF